AF425723

In July, on the fourth day it was, Jay the Jazz Playing Jaguar created so much buzz.

Come one come all join in on the fun, let's jam until the night is done.

The word is all over Animal Park, and the stage is set for the fun to start.

As fireworks hit the air jungle friends
gathered around, to hear the joy of
jazz make such a lovely sound.

Jay played many instruments for he had the job of his dreams. He played the piano, cello, trombone, and saxophone. He could do so many things!

Sarah the snake was slithering on
the dance floor,

While Galaxy the gorilla chanted
more and more.

Mr. and Mrs. King watched with delight.

While Jason the jackrabbit screamed,
"Outta sight"!

JAY
WAY

The party is only beginning, Let Jay the Jazz Playing Jaguar juke you to a fun evening.

Did you see it?

Take a look back at some things you might have missed. Do you see it now?

Besides reading the story, how would you know it was the 4th of July? Did you see the Independence Day on the post?

The type of animal Mr. and Mrs. King are was never mentioned. Did you know who they were? Answer: Levy and Layla the "Lion Kings'.

Not only was Jay a Jaguar, but he also drove a Jaguar car. The car feature is a generated version of what the first Jaguar looked like.

About the Author

Hello! My name is J. Lyles and I first would like to thank you for taking the time to check out this wonderful book. I sincerely hope you will enjoy reading it and please share it with your family and friends. I am a professional educator, powerlifter, and entrepreneur. However, those jobs are not as important as being a father. My commitment to helping my children have a brighter future led me to write. I showcase that commitment with the illustrations of my family throughout my first book "Galaxy The Gigantic Gorilla". Continuing with that commitment I now bring you Jay the Jazz Playing Jaguar and His Jungle Friends. This short tale is full of J-letter site words spoken in an exciting and inspiring story. Again, with great pleasure, you have decided to check out the wonder tale of Jay the Jaguar putting on an exciting jazz party for his jungle friends.

J' Words Defined

Jaguar - is a large heavily built cat with a yellowish-brown coat with black spots.

Jam - to enjoy music by dancing

Jay - The letter "J" spelled out is used as a first name.

Jazz - v play or dance to music

Job - a task or piece of work

Join - link or connect

Joy - a happy feeling

Juke - dance in a rhythmic way.

July - the 7th month of the year.

Jump - to move suddenly and specifically in a quick way

Jungle - an area of land with overgrown trees and vegetation.

9798989185412